Introduction to the Stockmarket

Mark McIlroy

<u>Other books by the author</u>

The Wise Investor

The Art and Craft of Computer
Programming

SQL Essentials

These books are available in print from
Amazon.com

ISBN 978-1515103714

Edition 11

Contents

1. Investing in the stockmarket

The stockmarket is one of the five major asset classes for investment, the others being Property, Fixed Interest, Cash and Alternative Assets.

The stockmarket typically has a higher long term return that any of the other major asset classes, although this comes at the cost of higher volatility in prices.

Investing in the stockmarket involves buying shares.

Owning shares means that you are a shareholder and one of the owners of a company.

You are entitled to a share of the profits that a company generates and a share of the assets if it is wound up.

Most companies listed on a stock exchanges operate businesses.

However, there are also other types of shares and units that can be bought on stock exchanges and these are described in later chapters.

Share prices range from a few cents per share up to several hundred dollars per share.

Share prices cannot be directly compared to each other but are compared using ratios such as the PE ratio and Dividend Yield.

Investing in the stockmarket is best suited to long term returns.

The market has returned around 11% per annum over the last 100 years (including dividends), which is higher than any other major asset class.

However prices can fall by 5% in a day and up to 50% over a year.

A share price can fall to zero but you cannot be left owing more money than you paid for the share (this is known as Limited Liability).

2. Dividends

Dividends are one of the main reasons for investing in the stockmarket.

When a company makes a profit, as most do, it may pay out some of the profit to shareholders as a dividend.

This is received as a cash payment by the shareholder.

Dividends are usually paid twice a year.

The 'dividend yield' is the percentage return at the current share price.

Dividend yields are typically 2% to 3% but may be as high as 6%.

This is the annual dividend divided by the share price and is similar to the rate of interest on a bank account.

Stable companies with low earnings growth generally pay good dividends.

High growth companies may pay little or no dividends.

Dividends can be invested in new shares instead of being received in cash through a company's Dividend Reinvestment Plan.

However this can make tax calculations complex when it comes time to sell the shares.

3. Franking

In Australia, the government has introduced a system known as Dividend Imputation or Franking.

This means that investors receive a tax credit on dividends received equal to the tax that the company has paid.

The current company tax rate is 30%. This means that dividends receive a tax credit of 30%, i.e. if your marginal tax rate is 30% there is no tax to pay on the dividends.

If your tax rate is lower that 30% you receive a refund in cash from the tax office for the difference, and if it is more than 30% you only pay the excess over 30%.

This explanation is for Fully Franked dividends, some companies only pay partly franked or unfranked dividends.

4. IPO – Initial Public Offering

There are two ways to purchase shares.

Most commonly you will be buying shares from someone who wants to sell them, which is done through a stockbroker. This is known as the 'secondary market'

It is also possible to buy ('subscribe') for shares that are being listed by a company for the first time.

This is known as an IPO ('Initial Public Offering'), also known as the 'primary market'.

Over the last few decades in Australia, many enterprises that were formerly government owned, such as banks and airports, have been sold to the general public through IPO's.

5. Brokers

Stockbroking firms fulfill several roles within the finance industry.

One does not generally buy shares directly from another investor, 'buy' and 'sell' orders are placed with a stockbroking firm which matches them with a counterparty who is quoting the opposite trade on the exchange, during opening hours.

Also, some brokers provide research reports on companies which are listed on the exchange which investors can read and use to decide which shares to buy or sell.

6. Economics

Economics is the study of growth and production in the economy of a country.

The most important economic indicator is GDP or Gross Domestic Product.

GDP measures the total production of a country's economy.

This is usually reported as the growth over the previous year, in real terms (i.e. after inflation).

GDP growth is typically 3% for developed economies and up to 7% for emerging markets.

The rate of GDP growth has an important impact on company profits and interest rates.

When growth is high, the central bank will raise interest rates to slow the economy and prevent the outbreak of inflation.

When growth is low, the central bank lowers interest rates to stimulate growth and prevent a recession.

A recession is defined as two quarters of negative growth.

7. Diversification

It is very important when investing in shares to spread your money between a number of different investments.

It takes about 12 to 15 companies to reduce your risk to the risk of the overall market.

This is most easily achieved by selecting a diversified portfolio of 12 to 15 companies or by investing in a managed fund or index ETF.

8. Managed funds

When investing in a managed fund, your funds are pooled with other investor's money and managed by professional managers.

Investing in managed funds is the most effective way to reduce your risk to the risk of the overall market and avoid 'stock specific' risk.

However the disadvantage is that there are fees to pay to the managers.

These fees are deducted from your account, they are not billed separately.

Managed funds typically hold investments in 30 to 100 companies.

Management fees on managed funds are measured by the MER (Management Expense Ratio) or ICR (Indirect Cost Ratio).

MER's vary between 0.1% and 1.9% of the asset value of the fund, per annum.

You should be wary of any fund that has a high MER. In this case, the manager must earn at least the MER on average in excess return to simply match the broad market return.

9. Indexes

An index is a way of measuring the overall level of share prices.

Famous indexes include the Dow Jones Industrial Average and S&P 500 indexes in the United States and the All Ordinaries Index in Australia.

The index is an average level of share prices in a range of companies, ranging from 30 to 2000 companies depending on the index.

Most indexes are 'capitalisation weighted', which means that the percentage representation of a company in the index is dependent on its size.

The level of index values is widely quoted in the press.

10. Index Funds

An index fund is a fund that does not attempt to beat the overall market but simply provide the overall market return.

The index fund attempts to match the return on an index which is a measure of the overall stockmarket return.

The fees of index funds are generally lower than the fees of actively managed funds.

This can make a big difference to your overall return over the long term.

The affect of compounding returns means that a small difference in the annual return can translate into a large difference in the final value of an investment.

Index investing is also known as passive investing.

11. Financial Analysis

Financial Analysis of companies generally focuses on the financial statements, which are released twice a year.

The balance sheet records all the assets and liabilities (debts and other owings) at the balance date.

The financial statements are prepared according to national and international accounting standards to ensure that they can be compared between companies.

A high level of debt is a warning sign that the company is risky however this does not always become obvious until it is too late.

The Profit and Loss statement records all the income and expenses for the period.

12. Ratios

Analysis of companies generally uses ratios.

The most important ratio is the Price-Earnings ratio.

This is the ratio of the share price to the company's earnings.

PE ratios are generally around 15 but may be as high as 50 for high growth companies.

The PE level of the overall market is also reported in the press.

This is an extremely important indicator of the level of the overall market.

You should avoid investing in the stockmarket when the PE is at a high level. This is a sign that the market is overvalued and could be due for a crash.

Other ratios include the PNTA, the Price to Net Tangible Assets ratio. This compares the share price to the assets of the company. The measure of assets excludes intangible assets such as goodwill and media mastheads.

13. Research

It is possible for an investor to research companies listed on the stock exchange themselves by reading annual reports and researching the dynamics of the industry in which the company operates.

In practice, this is such a large task that it is beyond most people. Even institutional investors rely on research reports sourced from brokers.

There are several places that you can source research reports on companies that have been written by full-time share analysts.

If you are a client of a full-service broker, the broker will employ analysts to research companies and write research reports. These reports will be available to you. They would normally contain an overview of the company and its financials, along with a 'Buy', 'Hold' or 'Sell' recommendation.

Some brokers also list 'Strong Buy' and 'Strong Sell' recommendations.

Another source of research is investment newsletters, which tend to focus on smaller companies.

Investment newsletters are generally not free and cost several hundred dollars a year.

14. When to avoid the market

The stockmarket is subject to regular falls and even occasional crashes.

You can take a long term view of the market and invest during the highs and the lows.

Investing at regular intervals rather than in one lump sum is known as "dollar cost averaging" and can reduce the risk of investing in shares.

However, if you have a large lump sum to invest you should consider the overall level of the stockmarket before making an investment.

After several years of strong rises the market may become overvalued.

This may be an indication that a fall is due.

The overall level of the market is best measured by comparing the current market PE ratio to its historical average.

If the current overall market PE is well above its historical average, you should consider investing only part of your lump sum in shares.

These issues will be widely discussed in the press in economics articles.

An easier approach to assess the level of the market level is by comparing the dividend yield of the overall market and your selected shares against the yield available on other asset classes such as cash and property.

If the dividend yield on the market is well below the yield available on other asset classes, this may be an indication that it would be wise to avoid making additional share investments in the short term.

15. Recessions and bear markets

Economic recessions are a fact of life.

A recession is defined as two successive quarters of negative economic growth.

During a recession, many companies make annual losses and stop paying dividends.

The only real solution to investing during recessions is to be patient, and wait for the economy and stock prices to recover.

A 'bear market' is defined as a situation where share prices have fallen by 20% from their previous high.

Bear markets occur every few years and can last for a year or two.

The best protection against bear markets is to avoid investing in speculative stocks.

A speculative stock is a company that has explosive growth potential, but has little in the way of current earnings, assets or dividends.

While investing in speculative shares can be exciting, it's possible to loose all your money if the company fails to deliver on its promise, which is often what happens, or the stockmarket enters bear market territory.

16. Property trusts and Infrastructure

As well as shares in companies running businesses you can also buy units in investment trusts on the stock exchange.

These may invest in property (usually commercial property such as office buildings and shopping centres).

Your funds are pooled with other investors and used to buy properties.

This method is an effective way of investing in properties although you should be careful that the fund manager has not borrowed too much as this can lead to volatile performance and losses.

Also, units in infrastructure assets such as airports and toll roads are sometimes listed on stock exchanges.

17. EFTs

EFTs or Exchange Traded Funds are a modern development in the market.

These are investment funds with the units traded on a stock exchange.

ETF's are generally Index funds.

The fees are typically lower than other managed funds.

18. Charting

Charting, also called technical analysis, is one form of investment analysis that you will read about in the financial press.

Charting involves producing charts of share prices and looking for patterns in the prices.

Charting is widely used especially for commodities and foreign exchange.

Investors should exercise caution in following this approach.

There is little sustainable evidence that it is possible to outperform the general market by following this approach.

Charting may be most useful when looking at large deviations from fair-value that might occur on long-term timeframes.

19. Day-trading

Day-trading involves buying and selling shares on a daily basis.

This approach generates a lot of brokerage costs which reduces the investor's capital.

Like charting this approach should be used with caution.

20. Style investing – "value" and "growth" investing

Professional funds managers generally manage their portfolios according to an investment 'style'.

The academic research suggests that 'value' companies outperform other companies over the long term. This is particularly the case for smaller companies.

"Value" shares are share prices with low price-to-NTA and PE ratios.

Other managers look for companies with strong growth potential and invest in 'growth' companies.

21. Opening an account

To buy shares you will need to open an account with a stock broker, or invest through a managed fund or financial adviser.

Opening an account with a broker is generally free.

Brokerage rates have come down over recent years and it is possible to trade from $20 per trade.

The minimum amount required to invest in shares is generally a few thousand dollars.

Some brokers operate predominantly online and also through call centres.

22. Penny stocks

When investors are young they often start their investing career by investing a few thousand dollars in some 'penny stocks'.

These are small companies with share prices of less than a dollar, or possibly a few dollars per share.

Investing in these companies can be quite exciting because it is not uncommon for the share price to rise or fall by 20% or 30% in a single day.

The companies may be small mining companies, technology companies, services companies and so on.

These companies are well covered by the various investment newsletters available.

This process can be an effective learning experience.

23. Margin Lending

If you want to borrow money to invest in shares this can increase the long-term returns but also increases the risk

Money can be borrowed using a home or other property as security, or using a "margin loan"

A margin loan is available from stockbrokers for up to 70% of the value of the existing shares held.

This can triple the size of your investments.

The shares are held by the broker as security for the loan however you continue to receive all dividends.

If the value of the shares falls, additional cash must be put into the loan or some of the shares will be sold. This is known as a 'margin call.'

24. The Efficient Market Hypothesis

The Efficient Market Hypothesis is an academic theory relating to the stockmarket.

This theory states that share prices already have all known current information 'priced in' to their share price.

This means that future moves are random and that it is impossible to outperform the overall market by selecting individual companies for investment.

There is considerable academic evidence that the Efficient Market Hypothesis is correct, especially for larger companies.

On average, the average active medium and large capitalisation investment manager does not beat the broad market return, as measured by an index.

Also, managers that beat the index in one year have no statistical likelihood of beating the index in the next year.

This surprising result has serious implications for investors.

It suggests that index funds are the best investment as they offer the overall market return with lower fees than actively managed funds.

It should be noted that these results are not necessarily a reflection on the competence of the managers involved. It simply suggests that market pricing is efficient and opportunities for outperformance simply do not exist.

Also, the continued operation of an effective and efficient market relies on active managers continually researching and trading shares.

25. International Investment

Investing in shares need not be limited to your home country. Virtually all countries have stock exchanges.

Most overseas stockmarkets have similar features to the markets described in this book.

Tax arrangements vary from country to country. Also, the industry structure varies between countries. For example, Defense contractors and Pharmaceutical companies are major industries in the United States, however these industries are virtually unknown in Australia. In Australia the major banks and mining companies comprise a large percentage of the market.

Investing overseas has some complications. Your broker may take orders for the major overseas markets, however the tax situation may be complicated. These complications may be reduced by using ETF's traded on your local market, or managed funds.

When investing overseas you are exposed to currency risk. This means that, if the value of your home currency rises, the value of your overseas investments effectively falls, and vice versa.

Despite these problems, international share investment through managed funds or ETF's is recommended as it can further reduce the risk of share investment through diversifying away from your home country share investments.

26. Long term cycles

A vast amount of research has been conducted into long term and short term stockmarket cycles.

While much of this is inconclusive, one study of US share prices from 1925 to 2015 identified some interesting results.

According to this research, stock markets operate in regular cycles.

This involves share prices staying flat for 15 years, then rising steadily for 20 years.

This pattern then repeats.

The implications of this for investors are that you might hold shares that don't increase in price for periods of up to 15 years.

However, during these periods shares on average continue to pay steady dividends.

This result emphasizes that to be successfully in investing in the stockmarket, you need to be a long-term investor.

27. Structured products

Investment banks issue a range of products that combine debt, equity investment and possibly other features in a single investment.

These products may offer increased exposure to rises in share values, at the expense of higher losses if share prices fall.

Other products may be aimed at returning a higher income yield than investment directly into the major investment markets.

Some of these products offer attractive features to particular investors.

On the negative side, some products have a high exit cost depending on the nature and design of the product.

28. Sensationalist stories

There is always someone predicting that the market is about to crash. This is normal.

However, even if prices fall in the short to medium term, a diversified share portfolio should still produce a flow of dividends.

If the dividend yield on shares is well below the yield that is available on other asset classes such as shares and property, this may be a sign to avoid investing additional money in shares in the short term.

If the yield on shares matches or exceeds the yield available on other asset classes this should provide a margin of safety for new share investments.

Always keep an allocation to the other asset classes as well, being Property, Fixed Interest, Cash and Alternative Assets.

29. Conclusion

Overall, investment in the stock market can be one of the best long-term investments that an investor can make.

Investment in shares can be made with few entry or exit costs, and part or all of an investment can generally be liquidated on any day that the market is open.

Downsides of share investment include the fact that share prices can fall by 30% or 50% over the course of a few months.

Also, investors that spread their investment across a small number of companies or who trade frequently risk losing some or all of their capital.

Share investment it is particularly suitable for the long term accumulation of retirement savings, as these funds will be invested for a long period of time and can ride out the ups and downs of the market.

Diversification is important and this can best be achieved selecting a portfolio of at least 12 to 15 shares or by using managed funds or index funds.

Index funds and ETF's are attractive investments as they deliver the overall market return with lower fees.

30. About the author

Mark McIlroy has Masters degrees in Applied Finance and Financial Planning.

He also has an undergraduate degree in Computer Science and Applied Mathematics.

Mark is a graduate of the Company Director's Course with the Australian Institute of Company Directors.

Mark has extensive experience in the Financial Services sector, in roles including Portfolio Manager (Quantitative), managing quantitative equity portfolios on the equities investment desk of a major bank.

Mark lives with his wife in Melbourne, Australia.

31. Additional Resources

Additional resources are available on the author's personal website,

www.markmcilroy.com

Author: Mark McIlroy

Email: mark.mcilroy@outlook.com

Readers are welcome to send general questions.

32. Contacts

Printed in the USA. Published on the Create Space Independent Publishing Platform.

Additional copies of this book may be ordered from www.amazon.com

Readers are also welcome to send general questions.

Author: Mark McIlroy

Email: mark.mcilroy@outlook.com